Worship and Warfare

A Prayer Companion

Dick and Flo Webster

William Carey Library
Pasadena, California

Published by
William Carey Library
P.O. Box 40129
Pasadena, CA 91114
Telephone: (818) 798-0819

ISBN 0-87808-962-4

The Scripture quotations in this book are nearly all from the New International Version or the New American Standard Bible, and are used by permission. A few are from the Authorized King James Version or are the author's own paraphrase.

Cover illustration by Robert Ellis
Text graphics by Jone Bosch

Printed by Gilliland Printing, Inc., Arkansas City, Kansas

WORSHIP & WARFARE

Table of Contents

Introduction   v

WORSHIP AND PRAYER   **1**

The Names of God   1
The Attributes of God   3
Hymns, Choruses, and Psalms   5
Praying for Oneself   6
Praying for One's Ministry   9
Praying for Others   13
Examples of Prayer from Scripture   17
Answered Prayers in Scripture   19
Encouraging Scripture Promises   21
Commands that Can Help Me   23
Focusing on the Goodness of God   24
Conditions to Answered Prayer   26
Helpful Quotes   28

WARFARE INTERCESSION   **29**

Sword Verses and Passages   29
Challenges to Militant, Persistent Prayer   31
Sample Warfare Prayers   34
 I. For a Christian in Testing   34
 II. For God's Servant Entering Enemy Strongholds   35
 III. For the Lost, or a Christian Away from God   37
 IV. For a New Christian   38
 V. To Be Prayed by a New Christian   39
 VI. Using "David's Five Stones"   40

INTRODUCTION

Is your prayer life constantly bearing fresh fruit to His glory? Or do you feel, like many others, that it is the weakest part of your Christian life? God has promised in His Word, "I will make them joyful in My House of Prayer," and that is what He longs to do for you.

A fruit tree can picture the child of God, full of faith and with a healthy prayer life, the fruit of which constantly gives life and nourishment to all those around. What is the secret source? The **roots**. These are what keep our prayers from becoming shallow, weak and superficial.

The **Names** and **Attributes** of **God** are the tap roots. Have you tried using them in prayer, first worshipping Him and then in reaching out in prayer for others?

"Counselor"...(you could take this name and pray), "Father, Your Spirit is my Counselor today, and I worship You for Your wisdom and perfect understanding of my need and situation...Now today I claim for _____, my brother in Christ, the counsel of Your Spirit, that under His guidance he may work through his problem!"

Take them one at a time, maybe meditating on just one or two a day. Meditate on what God is like, and take a few minutes to enjoy and appreciate Him. Use the lists of God's Names and the chart of God's Attributes, and you'll never run out of ideas!

His **Promises** are the second cluster of roots for our faith. Someone has said that there are 5,000 promises in the Scriptures. Through these we can know with confidence that we're asking according to His will! Are your prayers for others and yourself timid and uncertain; do you wonder if you're asking amiss? You have a new adventure awaiting you as you begin to let the Holy Spirit teach you how to claim one promise at a time, pressing in with confidence that you are asking something which your Heavenly Father longs to bring about in that life or situation!

"THE WORD OF GOD IS CALLING ME TO THINGS THAT HAVE NOT YET HAPPENED."

Mark some of these promises as they become special to you! **Memorize** them so you can pray in the very words of Scripture. Move in, and pray more than a "casual," passing prayer. In the end you will "see the glory of God!" (Jn. 11:40).

The **Commands** of God are not meant to be a burden. They, too, are for our encouragement! Someone has said, "God's commands are His enablings." Whenever a general gives an order, it is understood that sufficient provision is included to carry it out. He will not ask us to do something He does not supply the strength to accomplish.

Other things are included in this Prayer Kit that have been helpful to us. You will add to them as you think creatively under the guidance of the Great Intercessor. Most important...**Set aside a time for prayer each day**, and give it high priority. Then you will personally experience His promise:

"DRAW NEAR TO GOD, AND HE WILL DRAW NEAR TO YOU."

Dick and Flo Webster
Compilers

WORSHIP AND PRAYER

THE NAMES OF GOD

Almighty, Awesome, Advocate, Abounding, Answerer, Adequate, Author, Authority, Anchor

Brother, Bridegroom, Blesser, Beloved, Burden-Bearer, Barrier-Breaker, Boundless, Bountiful, Bruised

Christ, Creator, Counselor, Captain, Conqueror, Companion, Cornerstone, Compassionate, Comforter, Crucified, Controller

Dwelling-Place, Destination, Deliverer, Defender, Delight, Desire, Door

Emmanuel, Enlightener, Expectation, Encourager, Example, Exalter, Examiner, Enduring, End, Enabler

Father, Friend, Fountain, Fire, Forgiving, Faithful, Fairest, Finisher

Guide, Guardian, Good, Great, Glorious, Gracious, Giver, Gardener

Holy, Highest, Hiding-Place, Helper, Head, Hope, Healer

I AM, Incarnate Word, Incomprehensible, Incomparable, Infinite, Infallible, Invincible, Indwelling, Intercessor

Judge, Just, Justifier, Jealous, Joy

King, Keeper, Kind, Key

Lamb of God, Lord, Light, Life, Love, Leader, Longsuffering, Lowly

Most High, Master, Mighty, Meek, Merciful, Measureless, Majesty, Mindful, Mountain-Mover

Nigh, New, Needed, Nourisher

Omniscient, Omnipresent, Omnipotent, Overcomer

Prophet, Priest, Prince of Peace, Physician, Patient, Protector, Provider, Preserver, Praiseworthy, Precious, Prize, Pardoning, Persistent, Pure, Prayer-Hearing, Potter

Quickener, Queller-of-Storms, Quietness

Redeemer, Resurrection, Refiner, Refuge, Righteous, Radiant, Reprover, Renewer, Ransom, Refresher, Rescuer, Rewarder, Ruler, Restorer, Rock, Rest, Rod, Rich

Servant, Savior, Shepherd, Sacrifice, Salvation, Satisfier, Source, Spring, Sanctifier, Stronghold, Strengthener, Sun, Shield, Steadfast, Sufficient, Skillful, Supreme, Shade, Star, Song, Seeker, Sovereign, Slow-to-Anger, Sanctuary, Stronger One

Triumphant, Transformer, Teacher, Treasure, Truth, Tender, Tower

Uncreated, Unchangeable, Undefeated, Unhurried, Unforgetting, Unfailing, Unhindered, Unwearied, Unlimited, Uniter, Uplifter, Upholder, Understanding

Vine, Vindicator, Vanquisher

Way, Water of Life, Wisdom, Wonderful, Wellspring, Worthy, Wise, Watcher

Yearning, Yoke-Fellow

Zealous

The Attributes of God

He Is	He is filled with	He is able to	He seeks to free me from
trustworthy	wonderful plans	provide my needs	pride
sympathetic	concern for me	grant wisdom	irresponsibility
patient with us	concern for my brother	break chains	cruelty
all-wise	resurrection life	open gates	unclean thoughts
always with me	unlimited resources	still storms	fear
feared by demons	means of renewal	make dry bones live	ingratitude
the bread of life	beauty	heal my blindness	unfaithfulness
my enabler	concern for my children	remind us	bondage
creative		empower	inferior offerings
ever-present		convince hearers	desecration
God of Abraham, Isaac and Jacob		move moutains	strange fire
King of Kings		listen to my prayer	presumption
Lord of Lords		renew our strength	idle criticism
		turn tragedy to blessing	idolatry
		deliver from temptation	hypocrisy
		prune	confusion
		use His Word	waste
		test our faith	greed
		chasten	divisions
		give ample rest	self-centeredness
		protect the simple	cowardice
		use me	lust
		solve every problem	complaining
			materialism
			doubting
			shallowness
			foolishness
			mediocrity
			hardness of heart
			self-pity
			unbelief

3

The Attributes of God

He desires

singing
cleanliness
law and order
spiritual hun-
    ger
fairness
repentance
reverence
our first and
    best
generosity
excellence
obedience
growth
humility
body life
my part in his
    plan
gentleness
self-discipline
faith in him
periods of
    quiet
waiting in His
    presence
thankfulness
earnest prayer
concern for
    others
expectation
fervent love
    for one an-
    other

He has declared

vengeance is His
the greatest is love
seeing Jesus is
    seeing God
only one way to
    heaven
what I sow I will
    reap
I need more than
    physical food
His living water
    quenches thirst
He will never
    forsake me
sowing in tears brings
    fruit
His ways are higher
    than ours
His word will not
    return void
there will be a judg-
    ment day
waiting on Him
    renews strength

He also . . .

understands me
keeps His promises
surrounds us with
    angels
knows the future
will evalutate my
    service
can use my weakness
will not leave us
    orphans
came to destroy
    Satan's work
has armies of
    angels to help us
accepts us where
    we are
takes us on from
    where we are
forgives when we
    confess
doesn't perfect us
    all at once
is preparing my
    eternal home
rewards service
    and love

4

Worship and Prayer Hymns and Choruses Which Instill Faith

Hymns

'Tis So Sweet to Trust In Jesus
Breathe on Me, Breath of God
I Need Thee Every Hour
Speak, Lord, in the Stillness
Come, Ye Disconsolate
My Faith Looks Up to Thee
What a Friend We Have In Jesus
Take the Name of Jesus with You
Trust and Obey
How Firm a Foundation
Jesus, I Come
Peace, Perfect Peace
Lord, I Have Shut the Door
Be Still, My Soul
O Worship the King

Choruses

Set My Spirit Free
He is Lord
Hallelujah
Let All That Is Within Me Cry Worthy
Bless the Lord, O My Soul
His Name Is Wonderful
Thou Art Worthy
I Will Sing of the Mercies of the Lord Forever
Oh, How I Love Jesus
God Is So Good
Because He Lives
My Jesus, I Love Thee
Faith, Mighty Faith
Faith Is the Victory
His Name Is Higher
Holy, Holy, Holy Is the Lord
All Hail, King Jesus!
We Have Come Into This Place
Majesty
Jesus, Name Above All Names
O Come, Let Us Adore Him
Thank You, Lord

PROMISES TO BE CLAIMED IN PRAYER
FOR ONE'S OWN NEEDS

A. General—Valid for all Christians

"I will instruct you and teach you in the way which you should go; I will counsel you with My eye upon you. Do not be as the horse or as the mule which have no understanding." Psalm 32:8-9

"The Lord is near to the brokenhearted, and saves those who are crushed in spirit. Many are the afflictions of the righteous, but the Lord delivers him out of them all." Psalm 34:18-19

"Delight yourself in the Lord, and He will give you the desires of your heart. Commit your way to the Lord, trust also in Him, and He will do it." Psalm 37:4-5

"For the Lord God is a sun and shield; the Lord gives grace and glory; no good thing does He withhold from those who walk uprightly." Psalm 84:11

"Blessed are those who hunger and thirst for righteousness, for they shall be filled." Matthew 5:6

"When you pray, go into your room, close the door and pray to your Father who is unseen. Then your Father, who sees what is done in secret, will reward you openly." Matthew 6:6

"Do not be anxious then saying, 'what shall we eat?' or 'what shall we drink?' or 'with what shall we clothe ourselves?'...for your heavenly Father knows that you need all those thing. But seek first His kingdom and His righteousness, and all these things shall be added to you." Matthew 6:31-33

"I say to you, keep asking and it shall be given to you; keep seeking and you shall keep finding; keep knocking and it shall be opened to you." Luke 11:9-10

"God has poured out His love into our hearts by the Holy Spirit, whom He has given us." Romans 5:8

"No temptation [trial] has overtaken you but such as is common to man; and God is faithful, who will not allow you to be tempted [tried] beyond what you are able, but with the temptation [trial] will provide the way of escape also, that you may be able to endure it." 1 Corinthians 10:13

"Therefore, my beloved brethren, be steadfast, immovable, always abounding in the work of the Lord, knowing that your toil is not in vain in the Lord." 1 Corinthians 15:58

"Be anxious for nothing, but in everything by prayer and supplication with thanksgiving let your requests be made known to God. And the peace of God, which surpasses all comprehension, shall guard your hearts and your minds in Christ Jesus." Philippians 4:6-7

"If any of you lacks wisdom, let him ask of God, who gives to all men generously and without reproach, and it shall be given to him. But let him ask in faith without doubting." James 1:5-6

"Draw near to God, and He will draw near to you." James 4:8

"After you have suffered for a little, the God of all grace, who called you to His eternal glory in Christ, will Himself stablish, strengthen and settle you." 1 Peter 5:10

"If we confess our sins, He is faithful and righteous to forgive us our sins and to cleanse us from all unrighteousness." 1 John 1:9

B. Special—To Specific Persons in Scripture

"Have I not commanded you? Be strong and courageous! Do not tremble or be dismayed, for the Lord your God is with you wherever you go." Joshua 1:9

"Do not fear or be dismayed because of the great multitude, for the battle is not yours, but God's." 2 Chronicles 20:15

"'Do not fear...I will help you,' declares the LORD, 'and your Redeemer is the Holy One of Israel. Behold, I have made you a new, sharp threshing sledge with double edges; you will thresh the mountains, and pulverize them, and will make the hills like chaff.'" Isaiah 41:15

"When you pass through the waters, I will be with you, and through the rivers, they will not overflow you. When you walk through the fire, you will not be scorched, nor will the flame burn you." Isaiah 43:2

"I will pour water upon him that is thirsty, and floods upon the dry ground; I will pour My Spirit upon your seed, and My blessing upon your offspring." Isaiah 44:3

"I will go before you and make the rough places smooth; I will shatter the doors of bronze, and cut through the iron bars." Isaiah 45:2

"Even to your old age, I shall be the same, and even to your graying years I shall bear you. I have made you, and I shall carry you, and I shall bear you, and I shall deliver you." Isaiah 46:4

"Enlarge the place of your tent. Stretch out the curtains of your dwellings, spare not, lengthen your cords, and strengthen your pegs. For you will spread abroad to the right and to the left. And your descendants will possess nations, and they will resettle the desolate cities." Isaiah 54:2-4

"And my God shall supply all your needs according to His riches in glory in Christ Jesus." Philippians 4:19

PROMISES TO BE CLAIMED IN PRAYER
(For our Ministry)

A. General—Valid for all Christians

"Those who sow in tears shall reap with joy." Psalm 126:5

"The Everlasting God, the LORD, the Creator of the ends of the earth, does not become weary or tired. His understanding is inscrutable. He gives strength to the weary, and to him who lacks might He increases power." Isaiah 40:28-29

"Though youths grow weary and tired, and vigorous young men stumble badly, yet those who wait for the LORD will gain new strength. They will mount up with wings like eagles, they will run and not get tired, they will walk and not become weary." Isaiah 40:30-31

"Those who hopefully wait for Me will not be put to shame." Isaiah 49:23

"For as the rain and the snow come down from heaven, and do not return there without watering the earth, and making it bear and sprout, and furnishing seed to the sower and bread to the eater; so shall My Word be which goes forth from My mouth; it shall not return to Me empty, without accomplishing what I desire, and without succeeding in the matter for which I sent it." Isaiah 55:10-11

"I am with you always [all the days] even to the end of the age." Matthew 28:20

"If any man thirst, let him come unto Me and drink. And he that believeth on Me, as the scripture has said, out of his innermost being shall flow rivers of living water." John 7:37,38

"When He puts forth all His own, He goes before them; and the sheep follow Him for they know His voice." John 10:4

"If ye ask anything in My name, I will do it." John 14:14

"I will not leave you orphans." John 14:18

"You did not choose Me, but I chose you, and appointed you, that you should go and bear fruit, and that your fruit should remain, that whatever you ask of the Father in My name, He may give it to you." John 15:16

"You shall receive power when the Holy Spirit has come upon you." Acts 1:8

"Let us therefore draw near with confidence to the throne of grace, that we may receive mercy and find grace to help in time of need." Hebrews 4:16

"This is the assurance we have in approaching God, that if we ask anything according to His will, He hears us. And if we know that He hears us—we know that we have what we asked of Him." 1 John 5:14-15

B. Special—Given to Specific Persons in Scripture

"A fruitful bough by a spring; its branches run over a wall." Genesis 49:22

"Go, and I, even I will be with your mouth, and teach you what you are to say." Exodus 4:12

"My presence shall go with you, and I will give you rest." Exodus 33:14

"The Sovereign Lord has given me an instructed tongue,
To know the word that sustains the weary.
He wakens me morning by morning,
Wakens my ear to listen like one being taught." Isaiah 50:4

"I, even I, am He who comforts you.
Who are you that you are afraid of man who dies,
And of the son of man who is made like grass;
That you have forgotten the Lord your Maker,
Who stretched out the heavens,
And laid the foundations of the earth;
That you fear continually all day long because of the fury of the oppressor, as he makes ready to destroy?
But where is the fury of the oppressor?" Isaiah 51:12-13

"'For the mountains may be removed and the hills may shake,
But My lovingkindness will not be removed from you.
And My covenant of peace will not be shaken,'
Says the LORD who has compassion on you.
'No weapon that is formed against you shall prosper;
And every tongue that accuses [rises against] you in judgment you will condemn.
This is the heritage of the servants of the LORD,
And their vindication is from Me,' declares the LORD." Isaiah 54:10,17

"The Spirit of the Lord God is upon me,
Because the Lord has anointed me
To bring good news to the afflicted;
He has sent me to bind up the brokenhearted,
To proclaim liberty to captives,
And freedom to prisoners;
To proclaim the favorable year of the Lord,
And the day of vengeance of our God;
To comfort all who mourn,
To grant those who mourn in Zion,
Giving them a garland instead of ashes,
The oil of gladness instead of mourning,
The mantle of praise instead of a spirit of despair.
So they will be called oaks of righteousness,
The planting of the Lord, that He may be glorified." Isaiah 61:1-3

11

"Call to Me, and I will answer you, and I will show you great and mighty things, which you do not know." Jeremiah 33:3

"Did I not say to you, if you believe, you will see the glory of God?" John 11:40

PROMISES TO BE CLAIMED
IN PRAYING FOR PEOPLE

A. For the Lost, and Christians out of Fellowship with their Father

"I will keep you and will make you to be a covenant for the people...to say to the captives, 'Come out,' and to those in darkness, 'Be free.'" Isaiah 49:8-9

"'Can the prey be taken from the mighty man,
Or the captives of a tyrant be rescued?'
'Surely,' thus says the LORD,
'Even the captives of the mighty man will be taken away, And the prey of the tyrant will be rescued;
For I will contend with the one who contends with you And I will save your sons. And all flesh will know that I the LORD am your Savior, and your Redeemer, the Mighty One of Jacob.'" Isaiah 49:24-26

"The one in chains will soon be set free, and will not die in the dungeon, nor will his bread be lacking!" Isaiah 51:14

"You who remind the Lord, take no rest for yourselves; and give Him no rest until He establishes and makes _____ a praise in the earth." Isaiash 62:6-7

"How can I give you up, O ...? How can I surrender you, O ...? My heart is turned over within me. All my compassions are kindled." Hosea 11:8

"'Who then can be saved?'... 'All things are possible with God.'" Mark 10:26-27

"'...He has sent Me to proclaim release to the captives,
And recovery of sight to the blind,
To set free those who are downtrodden.'" Luke 4:18

13

"The Son of Man has come to seek and to save that which was lost." Luke 19:10

"Simon, Simon, behold Satan has demanded permission to sift you like wheat; but I have prayed for you, that your faith may not fail; and you, when once you have turned again, strengthen your brothers." Luke 22:31-32

"I came into this world, that those who do not see may see." John 9:39

"I have come that they might have life, and have it abundantly." John 10:10

"But the Counselor, the Holy Spirit, whom the Father will send in My name, He will teach you all things, and bring to your remembrance all that I have said to you." John 14:26

"The Helper...will convince the world of sin and of righteousness and of judgment." John 16:8

"Casting down imaginations, and every high thing that exalteth itself against the knowledge of God, and bringing into captivity every thought to the obedience of Christ..." 2 Corinthians 10:5

"Thou didst purchase for God with Thy blood, men from every tribe and tongue and people and nation." Revelation 5:9

B. For Christians in Stress

"Let the beloved of the LORD rest secure in Him, for He shields him all day long, and the one the LORD loves rests between His shoulders." Deuteronomy 33:12

"A bruised reed He will not break, and a dimly burning wick He will not extinguish." Isaiah 42:3

"When you pass through the waters, I will be with you, and through the rivers, they will not overflow you. When you walk through the fire, you will not be scorched, nor will the flame burn you." Isaiah 43:2

"The Lord is a refuge for the oppressed, a stronghold in times of trouble. Those who know Your name will trust in You, for You, Lord, have never forsaken those who seek You." Psalm 9:9,10

"Come to Me, all you who are weary and burdened, and I will give you rest. Take My yoke upon you and learn from Me, for I am gentle and humble in heart, and you will find rest for your souls. For My yoke is easy and My burden is light." Matthew 11:28,29

"And we know that God causes all things to work together for good to those who love God, to those who are called according to His purpose. For whom He foreknew, He also predestined to become conformed to the image of His son." Romans 8:28-29

"And stand he will, for the Lord is able to make him stand." Romans 14:4

"Being confident of this very thing, that He who began a good work in you will perfect it until the day of Jesus Christ." Philippians 1:6

"And my God shall supply every need of yours according to His riches in glory in Christ Jesus." Philippians 4:19

"I know whom I have believed, and I am convinced that He is able to guard what I have entrusted to Him until that day." 2 Timothy 1:12

See also, on Page 10 and 11: Psalm 34:18,19, 1 Corinthians 10:13, 1 Peter 5:10

C. Specific Promises for Family

"His faithfulness to His gracious promises is to children's children, to those who keep His covenant, and who remember His precepts to do them." Psalm 103:17,18

"Blessed is the man who fears the LORD, who finds great delight in His commands. His children will be mighty in the land; each generation of the upright will be blessed." Psalm 112:1-2

"He blesses the home of the righteous." Proverbs 3:33

"The tent of the upright will flourish." Proverbs 14:11

"The house of the righteous stands firm." Proverbs 12:7

"For I will pour water on the thirsty land, and streams on the dry ground. I will pour out My Spirit on your offspring, and My blessing on your descendants...This one will say, 'I am the LORD'S,' and another will write on his hand, 'Belonging to the LORD.'" Isaiah 44:3,5

"And all your sons will be taught of the Lord; and the well-being of your children will be great." Isaiah 54:13

"All who see them will recognize them, because they are the offspring whom the LORD has blessed." Isaiah 61:9b

"And I will give them one heart and one way, that they may fear Me always, for their own good, and for the good of their children after them." Jeremiah 32:39

(Also Isaiah 49:24-26 in section A.)

PRAYERS IN SCRIPTURE WHICH I MAY USE

A. For My Own Needs

"I will not let You go unless You bless me." Genesis 32:26

"If I have found favor in Your eyes, teach me Your ways so that I may know You, and continue to find favor with You." Exodus 33:13

"Are You not the God who is in heaven? You rule over all the kingdoms of the nations. Power and might are in Your hand." 2 Chronicles 20:6

"O Lord, let Your ear be attentive to the prayer of this Your servant and to the prayer of Your servants who delight in revering Your name. Give Your servant success today by granting him favor in the presence of this man." Nehemiah. 1:11

"I will lie down and sleep in peace, for You alone, O Lord, make me dwell in safety." Psalm 4:8

"I call to the Lord who is worthy of praise, and I am saved from my enemies." Psalm 18:3

"Show me Your ways, O Lord, teach me Your paths." Psalm 25:4

"May the words of my mouth and the meditation of my heart be pleasing in Your sight, O Lord, my Rock and my Redeemer." Psalm 19:14

"I will say of the Lord, 'He is my refuge and my fortress, my God, in whom I trust.'" Psalm 91:2

"Search me, O God, and know my heart; Try me and know my anxious thoughts; And see if there be any hurtful way in me, (say that causes You pain) And lead me in the everlasting way." Psalm. 139:23-24

B. For the Needs of Others

"Father, forgive them, for they do not know what they are doing." Luke 23:34

"May the God of hope fill you with all joy and peace as you trust in Him, so that you may overflow with hope by the power of the Holy Spirit." Romans 15:13

"But thanks be to God, who always leads us in His triumph in Christ, and manifests through us the sweet aroma of the knowledge of Him in every place." 2 Corinthians 2:14

"I am again in travail until Christ be formed in you." Galatians 4:19

"May God give you the Spirit of wisdom and revelation, so that you may know Him better." Ephesians 1:17

"That He would grant you, according to the riches of His glory, to be strengthened with power through His Spirit in the inner man." Ephesians 3:16

"And this is my prayer, that your love may abound more and more in knowledge and depth of insight." Philippians 1:9

"Praying for you, and asking God to fill you with the knowledge of His will through all spiritual wisdom and understanding." Colossians 1:9

"May God himself, the God of peace, sanctify you through and through. May your whole spirit, soul and body be kept blameless at the coming of our Lord Jesus Christ." 1 Thessalonians 5:23

ANSWERED PRAYERS IN SCRIPTURE
WHICH BOLSTER FAITH

"And Moses stretched out his hand over the sea; and the Lord caused the sea to go back by a strong east wind all that night, and made the sea dry land, and the waters were divided." Exodus 14:21

"And it came to pass, when Moses held up his hand that Israel prevailed; and when he let down his hand, Amalek prevailed." Exodus 17:11

"So the sun stood still in the midst of heaven, and hasted not to go down about a whole day...The Lord hearkened unto the voice of a man." Joshua 10:13-14

"And Elisha prayed, and said, 'Lord, I pray, open his eyes, that he may see,' and the Lord opened the eyes of the young man; and he saw, and behold, the mountain was full of horses and chariots of fire round about Elisha." 2 Kings 6:17

"They were helped...because they cried out to Him during the battle." 1 Chronicles 5:20

"And then they cried out to You again, You heard from heaven, and in Your compassion You delivered them time after time." Nehemiah 9:28

"And the Lord turned the captivity of Job, when he prayed for his friends; also the Lord gave Job twice as much as he had before." Job 42:10

"You hear, O Lord, the desire of the afflicted; You encourage them, and You listen to their cry." Psalm 10:17

"This poor man cried, and the Lord heard him, and saved him out of all his troubles." Psalm 34:6

"I love the Lord, because He has heard my voice and my supplications." Psalm 116:1

"'Our God whom we serve is able to deliver us from the burning fiery furnace, and He will deliver us out of your hand, O King.'...He answered and said, 'Look, I see four men loose, walking in the midst of the fire and they have no hurt.'" Daniel 3:17,25

"Now when Daniel knew that the writing was signed, he went into his house; and his windows being opened in his chamber toward Jerusalem, he kneeled upon his knees three times a day, and prayed, and gave thanks before his God, as he did before...Then said Daniel unto the king, 'O King, live forever. My God has sent His angel, and has shut the lions' mouths, that they have not hurt me.'" Daniel 6:10,21,22

"Then said he unto me, 'Fear not, Daniel, for from the first day that you set your heart to understand, and to chasten yourself before God, your words were heard.'" Daniel 10:12

"And Jesus lifted up His eyes and said, 'Father, I thank You that You have heard me. And I know that You hear me always.'" John 11:41-42

"Peter was kept in prison, but the church was earnestly praying to God for him...Suddenly an angel of the Lord appeared, and a light shone in the cell...and his chains fell off." Acts 12:5,7

"By faith the walls of Jericho fell down, after they were compassed seven days." Hebrews 11:30

OTHER ENCOURAGEMENTS
WHICH STRENGTHEN FAITH

"And God said to Moses, 'Remove the shoes from your feet, for the place on which you are standing is holy ground.'" Exodus 3:5

"He touched me again and strengthened me." Daniel 10:18

"Be strong and let your heart take courage, all you who hope in [wait for] the Lord." Psalm 31:24

"God is our refuge and strength, an ever-present help in trouble. Therefore we will not fear though the earth should change, and though the mountains slip into the heart of the sea." Psalm 46:1-2

"Be still and know that I am God." Psalm 46:10

"Cast your burden [what He has given you] upon the Lord and He will sustain you. He will never allow the righteous to be shaken [totter]." Psalm 55:2

"Blessed be Jehovah God...who only does wonderful things." Psalm 72:18

"Man's futile wrath will bring you glory. You will use it as an ornament." Psalm 76:10

"The mountains melted like wax at the presence of the Lord." Psalm 97:5

"I will open rivers on the bare heights, and springs in the midst of the valleys; I will make the wilderness a pool of water, and the dry land fountains of water." Isaiah 41:18

"As the heavens are higher than the earth, so are My ways higher than your ways, and My thoughts higher than Your thoughts." Isaiah 55:9

"I know the plans I have for you, declares the Lord, plans for welfare and not for calamity, to give you a future and a hope...and you will seek Me and find Me, when you search for Me with all your heart." Jeremiah 29:11,13

"Ah, Sovereign Lord, You have made the heavens and the earth by Your great power and outstretched arm. Nothing is too hard for You. 'I am the Lord, the God of all mankind. Is anything too hard for Me?'" Jeremiah 32:17,27

"'Do you not remember, when I broke the five loaves for the five thousand, how many large baskets full of broken pieces you picked up?' They said unto Him, 'Twelve.' 'And when I broke the seven for the four thousand, how many basketfuls of broken pieces did you pick up?' And they said to Him, 'Seven.'" Mark 8:18-20

"...He would grant you according to the riches of His glory, to be strengthened with power through His Spirit in the inner man." Ephesians 3:16

"Now to Him who is able to do exceeding abundantly (above) beyond all that we ask or think, according to the power that works within us." Ephesians 3:20

"Let us draw near with a sincere heart in full assurance of faith." Hebrews 10:22

"Do not cast away your confidence; it will be richly rewarded." Hebrews 10:35

"Is anyone of you in trouble? He should pray." James 5:13

"He prayed again [the seventh time] and the sky poured rain, and the earth produced its fruit." James 5:18

COMMANDS TO BE EMPLOYED IN PRAYER

(God's commands are equivalent to promises in that they always assume provision. "God's commands are God's enablements.")

"Make disciples of all nations." Matthew 28:19

"Love your enemies; do good to those who hate you." Luke 6:27

"Beseech the Lord of the harvest to send out laborers into His harvest." Luke 10:2

"This I command you, that you love one another." John 15:17

"Be kind to one another, tender-hearted, forgiving each other, just as God in Christ also has forgiven you." Ephesians 4:32

"Be strong in the Lord, and in the strength of His might." Ephesians 6:10

"Rejoice in the Lord always; again I will say, 'Rejoice!'" Philippians 4:4

"Let the peace of Christ rule in your hearts..." Colossians 3:15

"Whatever you do, do your work heartily, as for the Lord rather than for men..." Colossians 3:23

"Consider it all joy, my brethren, when you encounter various trials..." James 1:2

FOCUSING ON THE GOODNESS OF GOD

"Will not the Judge of all the earth do right?" Genesis 18:25

"God meant it for good." Genesis 50:20

"Keep the Lord's commandments and His statutes which I am commanding you today for your good." Deuteronomy 10:13

"The eyes of the Lord move to and fro throughout the earth that He may show Himself strong in behalf of those whose heart is completely His." 2 Chronicles 16:9

"How great is Your goodness which You have stored up for those who fear You, which You bestow in the sight of men on those who take refuge in You." Psalm 31:19

"O taste and see that the Lord is good; how blessed is the man who takes refuge in Him!" Psalm 34:8

"I would feed you with the finest of the wheat; and with honey from the rock I would satisfy you." Psalm 81:16

"You are forgiving and good, O Lord, abounding in love to all who call to You." Psalm 86:5

"The Lord is gracious and compassionate, slow to anger and rich in love. The Lord is good to all; He has compassion on all He has made." Psalm 145:8,9

"As the heavens are higher than the earth, so are My ways higher than your ways, and My thoughts than your thoughts." Isaiah 55:9

"Your heavenly Father knows that you need all these things..." Matthew 6:32

"But God demonstrates His own love toward us, in that while we were yet sinners, Christ died for us." Romans 5:8

"If God is for us, who can be against us? He who did not spare His own Son, but gave Him up for us all, how will He not also, along with Him, graciously give us all things?" Romans 8:31-32

GENERAL CONDITIONS TO ANSWERED PRAYER

1. A Cleansed and Obedient Heart
"If I regard iniquity in my heart, the Lord will not hear me."
Psalm 66:18

2. Acquaintance with His Will
"And this is the confidence which we have in Him, that if we ask according to His will, He hears us." 1 John 5:14,15

3. Simplicity
"But when you pray, do not be like the hypocrites...go into your room, close the door and pray to your Father, Who is unseen. Then your Father, who sees what is done in secret, will reward you openly." Matthew 6:5-6

4. Forgiveness
"And whenever you stand praying, forgive, if you have anything against anyone, so that your Father also Who is in heaven may forgive your transgressions." Mark 11:25

5. Love of Brethren
"And whatever we ask we receive from Him, because we keep His commandments and do the things that are pleasing in His sight. And this is His commandment, that we believe in the name of His Son Jesus Christ, and love one another, just as He commanded us." 1 John 3:22-23

"...fervently love one another from a clean heart." 1 Peter 1:22b

6. Humility
"God is opposed to the proud, but gives grace to the humble." 1 Peter 5:5

7. Diligent Perseverance

"Praying always with all prayer and supplication in the Spirit, and watching thereunto with all perseverance and supplication for all the saints." Eph. 6:18

(See also Luke 18:1-7)

HELPFUL QUOTES REGARDING PRAYER

"The great people of the earth today are the people who pray. I do not mean those who talk about prayer, nor those who say they believe in prayer, nor yet those who can explain about prayer; but I mean those people who take time and pray." S.D.Gordon

"Where prayer is focused, power falls."

"God's mercy seat is no mere stall by the roadside, where every careless passerby may put out an easy hand to snatch any glittering blessing that catches his eye."

"Intercession is man's highest calling."

"Prayer is the key that unlocks all the storehouses of God's infinite grace and power."

"The greatest thing anyone can do for God and man is to pray."

"Prayer is not overcoming God's reluctance; it is laying hold of God's willingness."

"Without God we cannot. Without us, God will not."

"When God says 'No' to my prayer, I can withdraw and stop asking, or I can ask 'why' and set out to learn through this experience."

"Battles are won only by the soldier who fights, and fighting involves using a weapon."

"Never tolerate in your heart the shadow of a doubt as to (1) the love of the Father's heart or (2) the power of the Father's arm."

"Who comes to Me an inch through doubtings dim... In blazing light do I approach a thousand miles to him."

"You'll never be a threat to Satan and his cause apart from prayer!"

WARFARE INTERCESSION

SWORD VERSES TO BE USED IN BATTLE

"And when they began singing and praising...the enemy was routed." 2 Chronicles 20:22

"Who is this King of glory? The Lord strong and mighty, the Lord mighty in battle. Lift up your heads, O you gates; lift them up, you ancient doors, that the King of glory may come in." Psalm 24:8,9

"So great is Your power that Your enemies cringe before You." Psalm 66:3

"Oh give us help against the adversary, for the help of man is worthless. Through God we shall do valiantly; and it is He who will tread down our adversaries." Psalm 108:12-13

"Fear thou not, for I am with thee; be not dismayed, for I am thy God. I will strengthen thee; yea, I will help thee; yea, I will uphold thee with My righteous right hand." Isaiah 41:10

"I will make rivers flow on barren heights, and springs within the valleys. I will turn the desert into pools of water, and the parched ground into springs...so that people may see and know, may consider and understand, that the hand of the LORD has done this." Isaiah 41:18,20

"I will go before you and will level the mountains; I will break down gates of bronze and cut through bars of iron. I will give you the treasures of darkness, riches stored in secret places, so that you may know that I am the LORD." Isaiah 45:2,3

"Be gone, Satan! For it is written..." Matthew 4:10

"All authority in heaven and on earth has been given to me." Matthew 28:18

"The God of peace will soon crush Satan under your feet." Romans 16:20

"For the weapons of our warfare are not the weapons of the world, but

mighty through God to the pulling down of strongholds." 2 Corinthians 10:4

"Be strong in the Lord, and in the strength of His might. Put on the
full armor of God, that you may be able to stand firm against the
schemes of the devil." Ephesians 6:10-11

"God exalted Him...that at the name of Jesus every knee should bow,
in heaven and on earth and under the earth." Philippians 2:10

"Having disarmed the powers and authorities, He made a public spec-
tacle of them, triumphing over them by the cross." Colossians 2:15

"Who by faith conquered kingdoms, performed acts of righteousness,
obtained promises, shut the mouths of lions, quenched the power of
fire, escaped the edge of the sword, from weakness were made strong,
became mighty in war, put foreign armies to flight." Hebrews 11:33-
34

"Resist the devil and he will flee from you." James 4:7

"The Son of God appeared for this purpose, that He might destroy the
works of the devil." 1 John 3:8

"Greater is He who is in you than he who is in the world." 1 John 4:4

(He said to me), "I hold the keys of death and Hades." Revelation 1:18

"They overcame him by the blood of the Lamb, and by the word of
their testimony; they did not love their lives so much as to shrink from
death." Revelation 12:11
"...The Lamb will overcome them because He is Lord of lords and
King of kings." Revelation 17:14b

CHALLENGES TO MILITANT, PERSISTENT PRAYER

"And when you go to war in your land against the adversary who attacks you, then you shall sound an alarm with the trumpets, that you may be remembered before the Lord your God, and be saved from your enemies." Numbers 10:9

"It is not by sword or spear that the Lord saves, for the battle is the Lord's." 1 Samuel 17:47

"'Answer me, O Lord, answer me, so these people will know that you, O Lord, are God, and that you are turning their hearts back again.' Then the fire of the Lord fell and burned up the sacrifice, the wood, the stones and the soil, and also licked up the water in the trench." 1 Kings 18:37-38

"In the name of our God we will set up our banners. May the LORD fulfill all your petitions." Psalm 20:5

"Who is the King of glory? The Lord strong and mighty, the Lord mighty in battle. The Lord of hosts, He is the King of glory." Psalm 24:8,10b

"The Lord will march out like a mighty man...and triumph over His enemies." Psalm 60:12

"The chariots of God are myriads, thousands upon thousands." Psalm 68:17

"Therefore He said that he would destroy them, had not Moses His chosen one stood in the breach before Him, to turn away His wrath from destroying them." Psalm 106:23

"And Hezekiah received the letter...and spread it before the Lord...Then the angel of the Lord went forth, and smote the camp of the Assyrians a hundred eighty-five thousand." Isaiah 37:14,36

"The LORD will go forth like a warrior, He will arouse His zeal like a man of war. He will utter a shout, yes, He will raise a war cry. He will prevail against His enemies." Isaiah 42:13

"And He saw that there was no man, and was astonished that there was no man to intercede." Isaiah 59:16

"And I looked and there was no one to help, and I was astonished that there was no one to uphold." Isaiah 63:5

"I searched for a man among them who should build up the wall and stand in the gap before Me for the land, that I should not destroy it; but I found no one." Ezekiel 22:30

"How can one enter into a strong man's house, and spoil his goods, except he first bind the strong man? And then he will plunder his house." Matthew 12:29

"And...upon this rock I will build My church, and the gates of Hades shall not overpower it. I will give you the keys of the kingdom of heaven; and whatever you shall bind on earth shall be bound in heaven, and whatever you shall loose on earth shall be loosed in heaven." Matthew 16:18-19

"And Jesus said unto them...'If you have faith as a grain of mustard seed, you shall say unto this mountain, 'Remove hence'...nothing shall be impossible...'" Matthew 17:20

"And He said unto them, 'This kind can come forth by nothing, but by prayer.'" Mark 9:29

"When a strong man, fully armed, guards his own palace, his goods are in peace; but when one stronger than he assails him, and overcomes him, he takes away his armor in which he trusted, and divides his spoil." Luke 11:21-22

"Men ought always to pray and not to faint." Luke 18:1

"And when they had prayed, the place was shaken." Acts 4:31

"Be on your guard; stand firm in the faith; be men of courage; be strong." 1 Corinthians 16:13

"Though we walk in the flesh, we do not war after the flesh, for the weapons of our warfare are not carnal, but mighty through God, to the pulling down of strongholds." 2 Corinthians 10:3-4

"That ye may know...what is the surpassing greatness of His power toward us who believe. These are in accordance with the working of the strength of His might which He brought about in Christ, when He raised Him from the dead, and seated Him at His right hand in the heavenly places." Ephesians 1:19-20

"For we are not contending against flesh and blood, but against the principalities, against the powers, against the world rulers of this present darkness, against the spiritual hosts of wickedness in the heavenly places." Ephesians 6:12

"Devote yourselves to prayer, keeping alert in it with an attitude of thanksgiving." Colossians 4:2

"Are they [angels] not all ministering spirits, sent forth to minister for them who shall be heirs of salvation?" Hebrews 1:14

"The effectual, fervent prayer of a righteous man availeth much." James 5:16b

SAMPLE WARFARE PRAYERS

I. WARFARE PRAYER FOR A CHRISTIAN IN TESTING

Heavenly Father, we are caught up in a fierce battle between Your forces and Satan's kingdom of darkness. First of all, today, we choose to focus our eyes on You Yourself, and Your goodness and beauty. There is no evil in You, and we praise You that we will *never* be disappointed in You! "How great is Your *goodness* which You have stored up for those who fear You, which You bestow in the sight of men on those who take refuge in You" (Ps. 31:19).

Today we come in behalf of _____, one of Your beloved children, who is in the midst of testing. Your desire is to use this trial to *bless* him, while Satan's desire is to use it to *defeat and destroy* him. In the authority of the Lord Jesus Christ, we bind all powers of darkness set on harming _____. We bind them aside and forbid them to work.

We invite Your Holy Spirit to enable Your child to join us in *welcoming* all Your purposes in allowing this trial, and *resisting and rejecting* all of Satan's purposes in it. We claim Your promise:

"And we know that God is able to make *all things* work together for good to those that love God, to them that are called according to His purpose, ...to be conformed to the image of His Son" (Rom. 8:28,29b).

We invite the Holy Spirit to reveal to _____ the "way out" which God has promised to provide for His children in every trial (1 Cor. 10:13). Whatever that "way out" is, whether *gratitude*, or *forgiveness*, or *praise*, or..., we ask that Your child shall see it clearly, and take it! We forbid Satan's forces to confuse the picture and cast doubt on Your *goodness*. We invite Your Spirit to lead _____ into Your Word, giving him a consciousness of *You* and *Your majesty* that far exceeds his awareness of all else.

We pray that through this trial, _____ will be purified and grow; glory will come to You; and every scheme of the enemy will be utterly defeated. "Many are the afflictions of the righteous, but the Lord delivers him out of them all" (Ps. 34:19).

We offer this prayer with praise and thanksgiving to You Who are worthy. In Jesus' name, Amen.

II. FOR GOD'S SERVANT ENTERING ENEMY STRONG-HOLDS

We bow before You our God, Lord of all the armies of heaven. Your name is Lord of Hosts, and we praise You, God of all the earth. You are worthy to receive all glory and honor and worship. Today we come to pray for _____, one of Your warriors. First, we invite your Holy Spirit to search our hearts, and reveal to us any sin, no matter how small, that would hinder this prayer. "Create in me a clean heart, O God, and renew a right spirit within me; *then* shall I teach sinners Thy ways, and sinners shall be converted unto Thee."

We thank and praise You for_____ who is willing to enter the line of the enemy's fire in order to take the gospel to those held captive by Satan. In the name of the Lord Jesus Christ we claim the protection of Your holy angels to guard and shield _____ today from the assaults of Satan's kingdom. In_____'s behalf, we lift up today the shield of faith, claiming Your word that *all* the darts of the Evil One will be quenched, and fall harmless to the ground. We count upon Your holy presence to surround _____ like a capsule, offering total protection for Your servant in body, mind, and spirit.

We claim for _____ today, in the authority of the Lord Jesus Christ, discernment to recognize and resist all attempts of Satan to *deceive, discourage,* or *defeat* in any way. We invite You to lead _____ into praise and worship, giving a consciousness of You and Your majesty that far exceeds _____'s awareness of the enemy or of problems he meets.

"I have set *the Lord* always before my face; because He is on my right hand, I shall not be moved" (Ps. 16:8).

We invite Your Holy Spirit to do His work of (1) filling _____'s heart and mouth with *Your Words* to speak, and (2) convicting those who hear of *sin, judgment,* and righteousness. In the authority of the Lord Jesus Christ, we use our spiritual weapons to smash and tear down every wrong thought and idea that prevents those who hear from *knowing Christ,* and understanding the truth of God (see 2 Cor. 10:3,4). We forbid Satan to snatch away the seed of God's Word that is sown in hearts today.

We join in the Psalmist's prayer in_____'s behalf: "O give us help against the adversary, for vain is the help of man. Through our God we shall do valiantly, and *He it is* who will tread down our adversaries" (Ps. 60: ll,12).

III. FOR THE LOST, OR A CHRISTIAN AWAY FROM GOD

Loving Heavenly Father, we bring before You in the name of the Lord Jesus Christ one who is very dear to You and to us, _____. Satan is blinding and binding him in awful bondage, and he will not come to You for help on his own. As priests of God, we stand in for him in intercessory prayer before Your throne.

In the name of the Lord Jesus Christ, we loose _____ from the bondage the powers of darkness are putting upon him. We ask for mercy and forgiveness for the sins of _____ by which he has grieved You. We lift up the cross of Jesus Christ, and claim back the ground of his life which he has given to Satan by believing the enemy's deception. In the authority of the Lord Jesus Christ, we resist all of Satan's activity to hold _____ in blindness and spiritual dullness. "Greater is He that is in you, than he that is in the world."

We invite Your Holy Spirit to open _____'s eyes of understanding. Remove all blindness and spiritual deafness from his heart. "The Holy Spirit shall convince the world of sin, and of judgment, and of righteousness." We "bring into captivity every thought to the obedience of Christ," so that _____ shall experience hunger, awakening, and conviction of all that pains You. We invite your Spirit to lead _____ into a (renewed) dedication to Jesus Christ as his Lord and Master.

We claim Your promises in Isaiah 49:

(for us) "Those who hopefully wait for Me *will not be put to shame.*"

(for _____) "Surely, thus says the LORD, 'Even the captives of the tyrant will be taken away, and the prey of the tyrant will be rescued; *For I will contend with the one who contends with you, and I will save your sons.*'

And all flesh will know that I, the LORD, am your Savior, and your Redeemer, the Mighty One of Jacob."

In the name of the Lord Jesus Christ, we thank You for Your answer. Grant us the grace to be persistent and faithful in our intercessions for _____, that You may be glorified in his life. Amen.

IV. FOR A NEW CHRISTIAN IN HEATHEN SURROUNDINGS

Loving Heavenly Father, I come to You in the name of the Lord Jesus Christ, and bring _____, one of Your children, before Your throne. He has received Christ as his Lord and Savior, and has become a child of God. But now You have allowed him to continue to live, for a time, where the powers of darkness are active, and where other people are deceived and held in bondage by Satan.

I bring _____ to You today, and thank You for Your protection over him in every area of his life. Show him today any sin or unwise action by which he has given Satan ground. Help him confess and turn from anything that grieves You. I thank You for Your promise: "He shall give His angels charge concerning you, to guard you in all your ways. They shall bear you up in their hands, lest you strike your foot against a stone" (Ps. 91:11,12). As the enemy seeks to *deceive*, to *discourage*, to *defeat* your child, I lift up the shield of faith, and in the authority of the Lord Jesus Christ I claim that every dart of the Wicked One will fall powerless to the ground.

Today I lift up the cross of Christ over _____, asking the Holy Spirit to cleanse his mind and thoughts toward those people (even members of his family) who are giving him pressure and trouble. I ask that You will set him free to *forgive*, to *love* these people, and to relate to them in the spirit of Christ. Grant him complete deliverance in every area of his life. "If the Son shall set you free, you shall be free indeed" (Jn. 8:36). Give _____ *courage* to obey You even in the face of opposition, sharing his faith with humility and wisdom supplied by Your Holy Spirit.

"Man shall not live by bread alone, but by every word that proceeds out of the mouth of God" (Matt. 4:4). I ask You to give _____ an increasing appetite for the Word of God, and an ever-deepening relationship with You in his prayer life. Bring some of Your children into his life who will encourage and instruct him. Keep him closely related to the Body of Christ.

I offer this prayer with thanksgiving to You, our omnipotent Lord, in the name of Jesus Christ. Amen.

V. TO BE PRAYED BY A NEW CHRISTIAN IN A NON-CHRISTIAN HOME

I come before you, my God, Creator of heaven and earth, the One True and Living God. I give You praise and thanksgiving. Through the grace of Your Son, Jesus Christ, I am an eternally forgiven child of God. He has redeemed me by His blood, and I bow in humble worship and willing submission to You.

By faith, I take my stand today with my Lord Jesus Christ, against Satan and his forces of evil. I draw near to my God and resist and refuse the devil any foothold in my mind and life. I claim the blood of Christ over my life, thoughts, and past, present and future sins [here it would be good to confess any known sin]. I choose to take up my cross and follow my Lord, even though it may mean my family will oppose me and though it may even cost me my life. I willingly offer myself as Your servant to share the gospel of Jesus Christ with my family. I claim Jesus' promise: "Whoever loses his life for My sake will find it" (see Matt. 10: 35-39).

Because You have rescued me from the power of darkness and brought me into the kingdom of Your beloved Son, I take my stand against any demonic influence that has come to me through my ancestors and family practices of false worship. In the authority of the Lord Jesus Christ, I reclaim all ground given to Satan in my life.

I acknowledge that You love my family and ask You to forgive them for their false worship practices and ignorance of Your truth and love. Cause Your light of the gospel to shine through my life today so that others of my family may trust in my Lord Jesus and become a part of Your eternal family. I ask You, Lord Jesus, to bind up all evil spirits that would oppress me and my family and remove them from my life and home. "For He has rescued us from the dominion of darkness and brought us into the kingdom of the Son He loves" (Col. 1:13).

"For as many as are led by the Spirit of God, they are the sons of God" (Rom. 8:14). Today I invite the Holy Spirit to lead and fill me, that I may live my life in all things for the glory of God. I praise You for Your promise: "My grace is sufficient for you, for My strength is made perfect in weakness" (2 Cor. 12:9). In Jesus' name, Amen.

VI. WARFARE USING "DAVID'S FIVE STONES"
(His Name, His Power, His Authority, His Cross, and His Glory)

In the *name* of the Lord Jesus Christ, the Son of God, Master of this universe and all that is in it, I come against you evil spirits, and all you are doing to hurt _____, (or to hinder God's work at _____). I command you all to go where the Lord Jesus would send you, for *it is written*: "God exalted Him to the highest place and gave Him the name that is above every name, that *at the name of Jesus* every knee should bow, in heaven and on earth and under the earth" (Phil. 2:9,10).

It is also written: "God raised us up (His children) with Christ and *seated us with Him* in the heavenly realms *in Christ Jesus* (Eph. 2:6). Therefore, even though I am unworthy, I am God's child and I am in Christ. I not only belong to His kingdom, but I have been seated with Him in His rulership, so I have been appointed to represent His name.

Likewise, *it is written* that, in our contending with you spirits of evil, we are to "be *strong* in the Lord, and in His *mighty power*." Therefore, I come against you spirits of _____, and according to His will and *His infinite power*, I bind all your operations against _____. In this conflict, all that has been bound in heaven I now bind on earth.

Again *it is written*: "He is the head over all rule and *authority*" (Col. 2:10). And when He appointed us to go and serve as His delegates, He declared: "*All authority* in heaven and on earth is given to Me...and surely *I am with you always*, to the very end of the age" (Mt. 28:18,20). On the basis of *His authority*, I forbid your attacks on _____to continue.

I also hold up against you the *cross* of the Lord Jesus, where He shed His blood for _____. For *it is written* that He "disarmed the powers and authorities...*triumphing over them by His cross*" (Col. 2:15). So you have no rights to harass and bombard God's children. I therefore insist that you cease all your attacks on _____.

And since *it is written* that "He has the name *King of Kings and Lord of Lords*" (Rev. 19:16), I also hold up before you His radiant glory, and I now worship Him as the highest, most majestic and worthy of all praise. I desire only His goodness to rule in all that concerns _____, so you must depart and proceed to wherever He would send you.